FAR OUT!
Exploring Nature
with Binoculars

Written by Christina Wilsdon
Illustrated by Dick Twinney and John Barber

Reader's Digest Children's Books™
Pleasantville, New York • Montréal, Québec

READER'S DIGEST CHILDREN'S BOOKS
Reader's Digest Road
Pleasantville, NY 10570-7000

Manufactured in China.
10 9 8 7 6 5 4 3 2

Library of Congress Cataloging-in-Publication Data

Wilsdon, Christina.
    Far out! : exploring nature with binoculars / written by Christina Wilsdon ; illustrated by Dick Twinney and John Barber.
        p. cm. — (Reader's Digest explorer guides)
    ISBN 1-57584-967-4 (paperback)
    1. Wildlife watching—Juvenile literature. 2. Nature study—Activity programs—Juvenile literature. 3. Binoculars—Juvenile literature. [1. Wildlife watching. 2. Nature study. 3. Binoculars.] I. Twinney, Dick, ill. II. Barber, John, ill. III. Title. IV. Series.

QL60 .W58 2000   590—dc21   00-028609

Introduction

"Look! What's that up in the tree?" your friend asks. You squint and peer up into the branches, but all you can see is a bulky shape.

Look up into that tree with binoculars, however, and you may find out just what that mystery creature is. Binoculars bring nature closer. Using binoculars, you can peer closely at a turtle on a log. You can watch a deer nibble on flowers. You can feel as if you are right in the nest of a bald eagle feeding fish to its young. In this book, you will find out how to use binoculars to explore nature. You'll also find out what there is to see in different places, or habitats, where animals live. Keep your eyes open for a hidden creature in each habitat, too!

How to Use Binoculars

Binoculars are a pair of telescopes placed side by side that help you look closely at far-off objects. Lenses in the binoculars make what you are seeing look larger—that is, they magnify what you see. The magnification power is printed on the binoculars. Binoculars that say "7 x" on them make the thing you're looking at appear seven times bigger.

Using binoculars is easy. First, look around without using them. Spot something with your eyes. Then, without looking away, lift the binoculars to your eyes with both hands. Adjust the wheel or little "seesaw" in the middle to focus.

If you can't find anything to look at with your eyes alone, try looking again with the binoculars. Move your head very, very slowly as you look at the scene from left to right. If you are looking at something tall, like a tree, look slowly side to side as you scan it from top to bottom.

Easy Does It

Holding binoculars steady while standing still can be hard. Try lying down or leaning against a rock or a tree as you look through them.

TAKE A BREAK
Peering through binoculars can tire your eyes. Rest your eyes by looking at the ground now and then.

I Spy

If you keep losing sight of an animal when you look through the binoculars, try this trick: Using just your eyes, find a big object, such as a large branch or a rock, that is near the animal you are trying to look at more closely. Then find that big object while looking through the binoculars.

Tips for Explorers

Exploring nature is no fun if you end up wet, cold, and totally lost! You'll enjoy it much more if you're well prepared. Don't go exploring alone. Take an adult and a friend along. Tell someone where you're going and when you'll be back.

Dress wisely. It's important to dress correctly for the season as well as the habitat you're visiting. If it's winter, bundle up. If you're visiting a marsh, wear waterproof boots. Wear clothes that are okay to get dirty and shoes with soles that have a good grip. Get permission from property owners before going on their land. Don't walk or climb in dangerous places. Don't try to touch wild animals or eat wild berries. And don't reach into holes—you never know what might be lying inside!

If you are exploring during hunting season, it is very important to wear bright clothes. Check with an adult about wearing special orange protective clothing and finding safe places to explore.

Pick a time when you are most likely to see wildlife. Many animals are more active at dawn and dusk. A few hours after dawn and early evening are good times, too.

Listen carefully. You may find an animal by hearing a rustle in the leaves or some other quiet sound.

Be a friend to other explorers—as well as to animals and plants—by leaving nature as you found it. Don't touch or remove nests. Put back any stones you turn over. And carry out your trash.

SLOW AND STEADY

While you're exploring, move slowly and quietly. Motion means "danger" to animals that are hunted by other animals. Many animals won't notice something that's not moving. Some animals don't see all the colors we see. A deer may not spot you even if you're dressed head to toe in red—but it may dash away if you scratch an itch!

Streams and Rivers

Fish, frogs, reptiles, birds, and many other animals live along the banks of streams and rivers. When you walk alongside one, look for animal tracks in the soft mud.

One animal in this scene is basking in the sun. Its colors help it blend into its surroundings. See if you can find it, then read more about it on page 11.

Deer nibble on the leaves and tender green branches of shrubs and low trees.

Red-osier dogwood

Bank Swallows

River otters eat fish, frogs, salamanders, and crayfish as well as mice.

Bullfrog

You may see an Osprey hovering over the water as it hunts.

Beavers build dams and lodges in streams. They enter and leave the lodges through underwater tunnels.

Green Heron

Splash! Belted Kingfishers dive headfirst into the water to catch fish.

Look for the Great Blue Heron wading in the water as it hunts for fish.

9

Walk along the bank of a river or stream and you'll find all kinds of animals to watch with your binoculars. Listen for the rattling call of the Belted Kingfisher. Look for an Osprey hovering overhead as it hunts for fish. If you're lucky, you might even see a beaver paddling by.

Great Blue Heron

The Great Blue Heron stands almost five feet (1.5 m) high. When it flies, it folds its neck into an S-shape, with its head nearly resting on its back.

Belted Kingfisher

The Belted Kingfisher's head has a fan of feathers called a crest. The female has a gray band across her breast and a brown band across her belly. The male has just one gray band.

Beaver

Do you see a branch being carried by the water? Take a closer look and see if it's actually being pulled by a beaver. You're most likely to see beavers swimming at dusk. Their flat, black tails don't show above the water as they paddle. But maybe you will see a beaver slap the water with its tail to warn other beavers of danger.

Beavers may grow to about four feet (1.2m) long and weigh up to 90 pounds (41 kg). They are the largest rodent in North America. To help them cut trees, they have two top and two bottom chisel-like teeth, which are always growing.

Osprey

Look for Osprey nests atop dead trees, telephone poles, or on nesting platforms people have built especially for them. Note the dark mask around the Osprey's eyes. This large bird has sharp spurs on its feet that help it hold onto the fish it catches.

Busy as a Beaver

Beavers use sticks, stones, and mud to build a dam. Water backs up behind the dam to make a pond. Then the beavers build a lodge to live in. They store food by jamming branches into the bottom of the pond. See if you can build a mini-dam.

What You'll Need

Mud

Sticks

Pebbles

Plastic washtub

Hose

What to Do

1. Build a dam out of the mud, sticks, and pebbles in the washtub. Use the mud as a kind of glue to hold the sticks and pebbles together.
2. Now run a trickle of water from a hose into the tub to test your dam. Does it hold water to form a pond? Or does it spring leaks?

Painted Turtle

Did you find this reptile hidden on page 8? Painted turtles live in shallow, slow-moving water. You may see several of them crowded on a log, basking in the sun. In the fall, these turtles burrow into the mud, where they spend the winter.

Bank Swallow

You may see this sparrow-sized bird with a brown collar zipping through the air after insects. Bank Swallows nest in large groups, so look for them if you see a steep bank covered with round nest holes.

Making Tracks

Take home a plaster cast of a track.

What You'll Need

Strip of cardboard
about 11 inches (28 cm) long

Paper clip

Plaster of paris mix

An old plastic container
(such as a gallon ice cream container)

Water

What to Do

1. Bend the cardboard to make a circle. Push the paper clip over the ends to keep them together.

2. Place the circle around a track as if you were framing it. Push it gently about a quarter inch (.6 cm) into the ground.

3. Mix plaster of paris and water in the container, following the directions on the box. Stir it with a stick. It should be as thick as pancake batter.

4. Pour it into the circle you made from cardboard. Let it sit for about an hour.

5. Carefully pull up the plaster cast and turn it over. After cleaning the cast, you can paint it if you like.

Pigeon

Rat

Deer

Watering Hole

If you don't have a stream in your backyard, try this trick to lure animals.

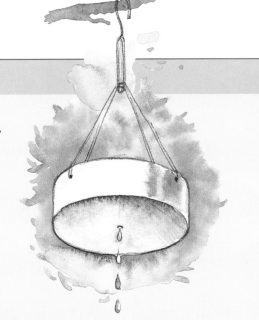

What You'll Need:

- Empty plastic food container
- 8–12 feet (2.4–3.6 m) of string
- Screwdriver or scissors
- Old garbage can lid
- Wire hanger

What to Do

1. Have an adult use the screwdriver or scissors to poke four holes just beneath the rim of the food container and one hole in the bottom (as shown in the picture).
2. Cut four strings of equal length. They should be at least 2 feet (61 cm) long. Tie a string to each of the four holes beneath the rim.
3. Ask an adult to squeeze the sides of the wire hanger until it's tall and thin with the hook at one end and a rounded loop at the other. Tie your four strings to the loop.
4. Choose a tree that is away from bushes where cats might hide. Hook the hanger over a branch so that the food container dangles a few feet above the ground.
5. Fill the container with water. Then put an upturned garbage can lid or other shallow container beneath it, on the ground. Put a small amount of water in the lid. Let the container's water drip into this puddle.

The dripping will attract thirsty birds and perhaps other animals. Keep an eye on things with your binoculars from inside the house or another hiding place. Take notes and identify the animals with your field guide. When the container is empty, pour the water from the lid into a bucket and use it to refill the container.

Tips on Toes

Many animals visit waterways to drink and feed.
Draw the tracks you find along the banks of a stream or river in your journal. Use a field guide to identify your tracks. Here are some common ones you may find.

Fox

American Coot

Freshwater Marsh

Over time, ponds may fill up with silt and dead plants, and turn into marshes. A freshwater marsh is home to turtles, frogs, insects, and many kinds of water birds.

One kind of water bird hides among the reeds, its bill pointed toward the sky. See if you can find it in this scene, then turn to page 17 to find out more about it.

American Coots

Blue-winged Teal

Male Red-winged Blackbirds flare their wing patches to warn other males away.

Canada Geese

Cattail

The Pied-billed Grebe builds a floating nest attached to plants.

Eastern garter snake

Green frog

You may spot a Northern Harrier flying low over the ground as it hunts for frogs, mice, and other small animals.

Mallards

See if you can spy the round nests of Marsh Wrens. These birds make nests out of cattail leaves and other water plants.

Bulrushes

Muskrats make their homes out of cattails, which they also eat.

Marsh rice rat

Marshes teem with life. Algae, tiny animal plankton, and fish thrive in the water. Insects fly, crawl, and swim in the marsh. Cattails, bulrushes, and reeds grow in the rich mud. Among these water plants live many kinds of birds, reptiles, rodents, and other animals.

Muskrat

A muskrat is much smaller than a beaver. Its long, thin tail is pointed, with flat sides, and sometimes sticks out of the water. Excellent swimmers, muskrats steer with their tail and use their partly webbed back feet to push themselves along. Muskrats can stay underwater for long periods of time. They are active day and night.

Canada Goose

Canada Geese have a black head and neck with a white chinstrap. You can hear their loud honking as they fly overhead in a V-shape. Canada Geese form pairs that may last for many years. The female lays up to 12 eggs, and both parents tend their young.

Seeing Red-Wings

Red-winged Blackbirds are noisy and easy to spot. See if you can find one of their nests. Then use your binoculars to keep an an eye on this nest throughout the nesting season. Look for the mother bird sitting on her eggs. How soon do the eggs hatch? When do the young ones leave the nest?

You can also try doing this with other bird nests you may find. (Be sure not to touch any of the nests or disturb the young or parents.) Record the activity you see. Write and illustrate a family history of the birds in your journal.

Pied-bill Grebe

Simply lifting your binoculars can frighten a grebe and send it diving underwater. This brown bird has a dark ring around its short bill. If it's hiding among plants, its bill may be the only thing you see.

Sneaking a Peek

It's hard to sneak up on frogs. They leap into the water with a "plop" if they sense danger. Binoculars are a great way to get a closer peek. Search around lily pads or along the water's edge. You may see just two eyes poking up above the surface.

Northern Harrier

This hawk's wings make a slight V-shape as it flies. It has a white patch above its tail. The brown female is bigger than the gray male.

American Bittern

Did you find this bird among the reeds on page 15? Its stripes help it blend in with the plants. If you spot one in the marsh, you may see it sway slowly from side to side—like the reeds waving in a breeze!

Home Tweet Home

Many birds nest in holes in banks, ledges, or trees. Here's an easy way to make a birdhouse of your own. Use your binoculars to see what kind of bird moves in.

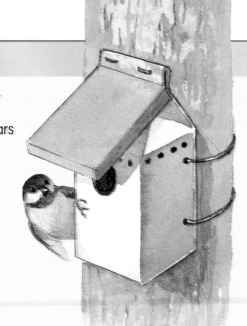

What You'll Need

    Clean half-gallon milk carton

    Scissors

    Shoebox lid

    Stapler

    4–6 feet (1.2–1.8 m) of heavy wire

    Wire clippers

What to Do

1. About three-quarters of the way up one side of the carton, cut a round hole about 1½ inches (3.8 cm) wide. This will be the front of your birdhouse.

2. Use the scissors to punch some little holes in the bottom of the carton. (These will let water drain out in case any rain gets inside.)

3. Punch four small air holes on each side just below where the top folds in.

4. Cut the shoebox lid to make a little roof for the house. It should hang an inch (2.5 cm) over the edge of the carton on all sides, as in the picture. Staple it to the top of the carton .

5. Poke two holes in opposite sides of the carton about 1 inch (2.5 cm) below the top fold. Do the same about 2 inches (5 cm) up from the bottom of the carton. Run 2 or 3 feet (.5–1 m) of wire through each pair of holes. (The length of the wire will depend on the size of the post or tree where you plan to attach your birdhouse.)

6. Now attach the birdhouse to a tree or a post that is in the shade, where it won't get too hot. Twist the wire around the tree or post to hold the house in place.

The Best Nest

Many marsh animals use grasses and other plant parts to build their homes. Why not provide nesting materials in your yard and see if any animals show up to "shop"?

What You'll Need

• A plastic fruit basket or mesh bag from the grocery store (strawberries are often sold in baskets; onions and potatoes are often sold in mesh bags)

• Nesting materials, such as fabric scraps, string, yarn, cellophane "grass," lint from the clothes dryer, hair from hair brushes or pet brushes, old pillow stuffing, cotton, thin strips of paper

• 1–2 feet (30–60 cm) of twine or heavy string

What to Do

1. Fill the bag or basket with the nesting materials.
2. Use the string to hang the bag or basket from a branch.
3. Use your binoculars to watch animals that visit. Note what they select. You are most likely to see birds, but squirrels may also visit. Watch the birds as they fly away and see if you can find out where they're nesting.

Mallard

You may see just the tails of these ducks sticking up as they dabble for food underwater! When they come up for air, you'll see that the male has a green head. The female is all brown. Mallards quack very loudly.

Duck, Dabble, and Dive

Watch how ducks take off from the water—it's a clue to how they eat! Ducks that leap up from the water and fly are "dabblers." They eat food off the water's surface or tip upside down to grub for food in the mud. Ducks that run across the water before taking off are usually "divers." They dive and swim underwater to catch fish.

Meadow

Meadows attract many kinds of animals. Deer come to graze on the grasses. Insects fly in to sip nectar from flowers. Songbirds feed on insects and seeds. Hawks swoop down on mice and voles that have grown plump on grass seeds.

Can you find a small brown-and-white bird? Turn to page 23 to learn more about it.

The Red-tailed Hawk catches voles and mice with its strong feet.

Eastern Bluebird

If you're lucky, you may spy a red fox looking for food.

Monarch butterflies only lay their eggs on milkweed.

Oxeye daisies

Turkey Vultures are nature's cleanup crew. They eat dead animals they find on the ground.

Grey birches

American Kestrel

Goldenrod

Woodchucks

Hognose snake

Horned Lark

The Grasshopper Sparrow is named after its voice. It buzzes like a grasshopper!

Yarrow

Meadow vole

The Meadowlark raises its young in a nest of grass on the ground.

21

Visit a meadow that's bordered by woods. Look for woodland birds or animals visiting the meadow. Walk along the trees where you will stand out less. Use your ears. Listen for the tinkling call of a Horned Lark or the hoarse scream of a Red-tailed Hawk. If a woodchuck sees you, it may give a sharp whistle as it runs for its burrow. If you're quick, you may spy it peeking out to see if the danger has passed.

Woodchuck
This brown, chubby mammal is about the size of a big, fat cat. It has a fuzzy tail and tiny ears. It spends most of the day above ground. Woodchucks spend winter in a deep sleep called hibernation.

WAKE UP
Have you ever heard of Groundhog Day? "Groundhog" is another name for the woodchuck. On February 2, woodchucks are said to come out of hibernation. If they see their shadow, they go back to sleep—and that means six more weeks of winter. The story isn't true, but you can honor the woodchuck anyway! Go outside on Groundhog Day and see if you can see your shadow.

Red-tailed Hawk
You will likely see this hawk soaring overhead or sitting in a tree at the meadow's edge. It has a red-orange tail and a "belt" of brown spots across its pale belly. If you see one hopping on the ground, it may be hunting for grasshoppers!

American Kestrel
This little falcon is the size of a robin. It often pumps its tail up and down while sitting on a branch. Kestrels also live in cities, where they hunt House Sparrows.

Flutter By

Try watching butterflies with your binoculars even if you are standing just a few feet away from them. You'll be able to see them closely without scaring them away. Watch the butterflies as they flit from flower to flower. Which color flowers do they seem to like the best? Keep track of this information in your journal.

Flower Power

Attract butterflies to your own garden or window ledge with flowers. Some easy-to-grow butterfly favorites are cosmos, daisies, yarrow, mint, phlox, asters, lobelia, sunflowers, marigolds, black-eyed susans, and lavender.

PLAYING TRICKS

Some kinds of animals protect themselves and their young by fooling other animals. A Killdeer, for example, pretends to have a broken wing if a hungry fox or other animal goes near its nest. It drags its wing and calls loudly to get the animal to follow it. Once its nest is safely out of range, the Killdeer quickly "gets better" and flies away!

Northern Bobwhite

Did you find the Northern Bobwhite on page 21? A bobwhite stands very still if danger is near. When it bursts into flight, its wings whir loudly. At night, bobwhites gather in a group called a covey. They form a circle, with each bird facing outward.

No matter what colors you wear or how quiet you are, birds and other animals are likely to spot you when you move. So people who study animals often hide in a structure called a blind. In a blind, you peer out through an eyehole and watch animals that don't know you're there! A pup tent can work as a blind. Even a jacket is useful. Instead of wearing your jacket, toss it over your head like a blanket and zip it up. Poke your binoculars out of the neck hole and be as still as you can.

You can also bring along an old sheet or a bedspread to use as a blind. Find several long, sturdy sticks and push them into the ground. Drape your sheet or bedspread over them. Leave a small opening in front to look through with your binoculars.

A large box painted brown makes a great blind if you can leave it in place after you set it up. See if you can snag a box that once held something big like a refrigerator—and set it up in your yard, a meadow, or a field.

Meadowlark

This bird has a yellow breast marked with a black V. It often perches on a post or shrub to sing its beautiful song. The Eastern and Western Meadowlarks look almost exactly the same—but they sing completely different songs.

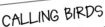

> **CALLING BIRDS**
> Lure birds into view by making squeaking sounds. Kissing the back of your hand loudly is a good way to do this. So is making noises like "Psh, psh!"

Watch the Birdy!

Keep an eye on the comings and goings of just one bird. You may be able to find out where it is nesting. Does it keep returning to a certain spot with food in its beak? Does it fly in a straight line? Or does it fly here and there, landing on grasses and seeming to take its time as it goes?

I Spy

Be a meadow detective. Look for signs of animal activity recorded in the grass. Can you find:

- A path through the grass that seems to be well-traveled? (Follow it and see where it leads.)

- A round, flattened area in the grass? (A deer may have lain here.)

- Feathers or footprints? (Sketch them in your journal.)

- A small bowl scraped out of the soil? (A rabbit may have slept here.)

- A series of small dirt piles? (This is the work of a mole.)

- Holes in the ground or on slopes? (Woodchucks, gophers, and other animals may have made these burrows.)

- Nests among the grass? (Many birds nest in tall grass—look, but don't touch!)

Eastern Oak-Hickory Forest

Animals can find lots of seeds to eat in oak-hickory forests. Squirrels carry acorns and nuts far and wide and bury them in different places. Some they eat in winter. The ones they miss will grow into new trees.

See if you can find a familiar small brown animal hiding in this scene. Then turn to page 29 and read more about it.

Scarlet Tanagers

Shagbark hickory

Black oak

Wild Turkeys scratch the ground with their feet to scrape up nuts and acorns.

Use your binoculars to see the Red-eyed Vireo's raspberry-red eyes! The male vireos sing like crazy in summer. One bird sang 22,197 songs in just 10 hours!

White-footed mice

Tufted Titmouse

Black-capped Chickadee

In spring, Hairy Woodpeckers drill nesting holes in trees. In fall, they drill roosting holes, where they sit or sleep.

Highbush blueberry

Be very still, and white-tailed deer may walk close to you without fear.

Look for the White-breasted Nuthatch on tree trunks. You may spot this small acrobat walking upside down, as it searches for insects in the bark.

White oak

Like squirrels, Blue Jays bury acorns in fall and dig them up in winter to eat them.

Gray squirrel

Most of the trees in an oak-hickory forest are deciduous. In the fall, the days get shorter and temperatures drop. This sets off changes that cause the leaves to turn bright colors. Soon after, the leaves will begin to fall, forming a deep carpet on the forest floor. In the spring, the trees will grow new leaves.

Raccoon

A raccoon has a black mask around its eyes and black rings around its tail. Its slim "fingers" help it feel for food in water— or turn doorknobs so it can sneak into cabins and find snacks.

White-tailed Deer

Male white-tailed deer grow antlers and are bigger than females. Fawns have spots. Frightened deer stamp their feet and snort loudly to warn other deer of danger. When they run away, they use their tails like flags to signal danger by flipping them up to show the white underneath.

Leaf Peeping

Pick a few trees in your area to watch as fall begins. Which ones change color? How does the color change—slowly or quickly, from the top or bottom? Can you find any patchy leaves that are part green and part red, yellow, brown, or orange? Write and draw your observations in your journal.

Headgear

If you see a buck, or male deer, with your binoculars, count the number of points on its antlers. Older bucks usually have bigger antlers with more points than younger bucks. Watch the way a deer's ears move as it looks and listens. What is it looking at? Can you find out with your binoculars? Is it looking at—you?

Wild Turkey

The Wild Turkey is very secretive. If you're careful, you may see this big bird in the early morning or late evening. You can hear its gobble a mile away!

Blue Jay

A Blue Jay may identify itself for you! Its loud call sounds like "jay, jay." A Blue Jay is about one foot (30 cm) long, and has a pointed crest on its head. Blue Jays chase and scream at owls or hawks flying by.

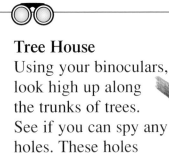

Tree House

Using your binoculars, look high up along the trunks of trees. See if you can spy any holes. These holes may be occupied by raccoons, squirrels, or other animals. If you see a hole, thump on the trunk of the tree. The animal may peer out to see what's going on.

Eastern Cottontail

Did you find this rabbit on page 27? Cottontails have up to four litters a year, with four or five young to a litter. To escape their enemies, they can swim, run up to 18 miles (30 km) per hour, and bound up to 15 feet (4.5 m).

29

Rose-breasted Grosbeak

White-breasted Nuthatch

The shape and size of a bird's beak are clues to what it eats. Birds that eat heavy seeds need short, strong beaks. Insect-eaters often have thin, sharp beaks for probing under bark and picking bugs off leaves. Woodpeckers have strong, sharp beaks for drilling holes in wood.

You may have household tools that work like birds' beaks. For example, a nutcracker works like a finch's bill. A needle-nose pliers works like an insect-eater's bill.

Hairy Woodpecker
The Hairy Woodpecker clings to the side of a tree, props itself up with its tail, and drums on wood with its beak. The drumming sounds like loud, fast tapping. You can tell the male by the red patch on the back of his head.

Scarlet Tanager
In summer, a male Scarlet Tanager is bright red. In fall, he turns the same color as the female—dull green. If you see one that's part red and part green—he's in between his summer and winter colors. His wings and tail are always black. Tanagers fly to South America for the winter.

BYE, BYE, BIRDIES

If you're a bird, it can be hard to find food in northern North America during winter. So many kinds of birds fly south in autumn to where it's warmer. Some may go as far as South America while others stop in the southern United States. Look up in the sky. Are there flocks of geese flying in a V as they migrate? Listen and you may hear them honking.

Tweet Treat

Nuts and seeds are rich in fat and protein. They are good foods for birds and other animals because they provide lots of energy. You can make an easy, nutritious snack called "suet" at home.

What You'll Need:

Medium-sized pot

Spoon

Beef lard (sold in packages in the meat section of grocery stores)

Birdseed (no exact amount is needed—2 or 3 cups will do)

3-foot-long (1 m) lengths of string

Small plastic containers such as old yogurt cups.

1. Ask an adult to melt the lard in the pot on the stove.
2. Let the melted lard cool a bit, then stir in the seeds. If you like, add about 1 pound (.5 kg) of oatmeal, raisins, dried fruit, and other tidbits for every ½ pound (.25 kg) of lard.
3. Pour the mix into the containers. Use the handle of a spoon to push one end of the string all the way down through the center of each batch. Tie a knot in the loose end of the string. Let mix cool and harden.
4. Remove the suet from the containers. Turn each one upside down and pull the string through until the knot rests against the suet. With the other end of the string, tie the suet to tree branches. Watch the birds that come to feed with your binoculars.

City Park

Would you believe that you can spy lots of wildlife in the city? Visit a city park and write down the different kinds of animals you see. If you eat lunch there, squirrels and pigeons may gather around you. Why? They're hoping for a handout!

Can you find a small reddish-brown animal with two white stripes in this scene? Turn to page 35 to read about it.

Crows

Active at night, raccoons may hole up in trees during the day.

Pin oak

Song Sparrow

Have you ever fed city pigeons? You will find them listed as Rock Doves in field guides.

American Robin

Peregrine Falcons

Look for gray squirrels running along power lines to get from place to place!

Ailanthus tree

Common Grackles

Gingko trees have been growing on Earth since the days of the dinosaurs.

Norway rat

House Wren

Mourning Doves

Starlings

House Sparrows

House mouse

In cities, wild animals have learned to live around people. Pigeons nest on windowsills and bridges. Peregrine Falcons build nests high on the ledges of tall buildings and prey on pigeons. Pigeons look for people to give them handouts. House Sparrows dart among the pigeons to get their share. Raccoons don't look for handouts, but raid garbage cans!

Gray Squirrel

A gray squirrel's bushy tail is as long as its body. Look for squirrels scampering along branches, fences, and power lines, or feeding on the ground. A squirrel buries nuts for winter use. If it catches you watching, it may just pretend to bury the nut. Then it will run away and find a new place to hide it!

SHADES OF GRAY

Some gray squirrels aren't gray at all. In the north, gray squirrels may be black. There are also groups, or "colonies," of white gray squirrels in Illinois, New Jersey, and South Carolina.

Nuts About Squirrels

Ask an adult to help you set up a trapeze for squirrels.

What You'll Need

6–8 feet (1.8–2.4 m) of rope
Twine or string
Peanuts

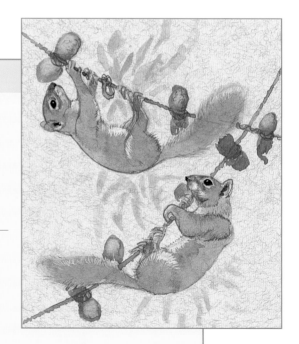

What to Do

1. Tie a rope from one tree branch to another at a height of about 5 feet (1.5 m) in a spot where people won't walk into it.
2. Use twine or string to tie the peanuts to the rope.
3. Watch with binoculars as squirrels walk across the rope and hang upside down to get at the peanuts.

Peregrine Falcon

The Peregrine Falcon is a gray bird about the size of a crow, with a dark cap and pointed wings. It also has dark "mustaches" around its hooked beak. A Peregrine Falcon can dive out of the sky at over 100 miles (160 km) per hour as it hunts for pigeons.

Starling

In spring and summer, a Starling is black with a shimmer of purple and green. Its bill is yellow. In fall and winter, a Starling's bill is brown, and its body is speckled with white dots. These dots are the white tips of new feathers. The millions of Starlings in North America came from just 100 birds brought from Europe and set free in New York City in 1890.

NEST SIGHTS

House Sparrow nests are loose, messy batches of grass and twigs. Sparrows like to nest in holes. In the city, a favorite nest site is inside the letters of neon signs!

Eastern Chipmunk

Did you find the chipmunk on page 32? Chipmunks eat insects as well as acorns, nuts, and seeds. These small animals have large pouches inside their cheeks. They use them to store food to take back to their nests.

Crow

Crows are black and may grow up to 20 inches (51 cm) long. They are very smart and will eat almost anything. If you're having a picnic, watch out! If you're not careful, a crow may steal your lunch! Crows also steal shiny objects and hide them.

American Robin

Dark gray with a reddish-orange breast, the male American Robin has a black head and tail. While some robins fly south for the winter, others stay in the north. In spring, the males fight each other for places to feed and nest. You may even see them fighting their own reflection in a window!

Scram!

Birds sometimes gang up on, or "mob," bigger birds that might harm their young. Look for small birds mobbing a crow or gull. Watch the action with your binoculars. Outside of a city, you can see crows mobbing very large birds, such as hawks, eagles, and owls.

Tug-of-Worm

Watch a robin as it pulls a worm from the ground. See how it tugs. Pulling up a worm is hard work because the worm hangs on with bristles all along its body.

Map It

Draw a map of your backyard or local park on a large sheet of paper or poster board. Show where trees, shrubs, and water sources are. Add to your map over time as you observe the wildlife that lives there. Can you:

- Pinpoint where certain squirrels live?
- Locate the burrow of a chipmunk?
- Show where you are most likely to see crows?
- Find a favorite roosting site of starlings?

As the trees drop their leaves in winter, can you see any nests left in the branches? Birds' nests look like little bowls left on the branches. Squirrels' nests are round bundles of leaves about the size of basketballs. Note which trees were favorite nesting sites.

Zoo Views

Is there a zoo in your town or park? Use your binoculars to watch the animals there. Get to know the individual animals in each exhibit by writing about them in your journal. Identify them by noting their special markings. This is how scientists studying groups of animals tell individuals apart.

Norway Rat

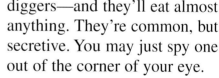

Rats live wherever there are people. They are good climbers and diggers—and they'll eat almost anything. They're common, but secretive. You may just spy one out of the corner of your eye.

Pine Forest

Pine trees are coniferous. They don't lose their leaves—or needles—in the fall. However, as new needles grow, old needles do die and fall off. Few plants can grow in the carpet of needles that covers the ground in a pine forest.

Look for a small brown bird creeping up a tree, searching for insects, then turn to page 41 and read about it.

Eastern white pines grow needles in bunches of five.

Purple Finch

The quaking aspen gets its name from the way its leaves tremble in the breeze.

Raven

Look for a Red-breasted Nuthatch creeping down a tree headfirst as it searches for insects.

Red squirrel

Porcupines sleep by day, so look for one snoozing up in a tree!

Red pine

Pine Siskins eat seeds—and sometimes the salt spread on highways to melt snow.

Golden-crowned Kinglets

A Red Crossbill often hangs upside down as it eats.

Winter Wrens

Jack pines grow needles in bundles of two.

Salt, Please!

Animals need salt in their diets—not to make their food taste good, but to help their bodies work well. People need salt, too. But while you can just say, "Pass the salt, please," animals sometimes have to search for salt. Porcupines like salt so much, they will even gnaw the wooden handles on tools to get the salt left behind by sweaty human hands!

Female

Male

Red Squirrel
The red squirrel is rust-colored with a white belly and fuzzy ears. In summer, it nips pinecones off trees and buries them in the ground to save for winter use. Look on logs and rocks for little piles of cone scales left behind from a meal. The red squirrel is also called a chickaree.

CHICKAREE CHATTER
Listen for a loud, long noise that sounds like "churrrr!" This is the sound of a red squirrel. See if you can spot the little noisemaker up in a tree.

Red Crossbill
Cross your fingers. That is what a Red Crossbill's beak looks like. Its odd shape helps the bird pry open cones. Then it uses its tongue to pull out the seeds. Only the male is red. The female is yellow-green. Sometimes Red Crossbills make nests and raise young in the middle of winter.

Porcupine

If you see a prickly ball perched high up in a tree, you've found a porcupine! A porcupine is covered with about 30,000 sharp quills. Few animals dare to bother a porcupine.

BARK AND BITE

Look up tree trunks for pale patches where bark has been torn away. These patches may be places where a porcupine has gnawed and eaten the bark.

Seeing in Snow

Bright light bouncing off snow can make it hard to see—with binoculars or without! Try making a pair of snow goggles.

What You'll Need

Piece of cardboard
(a shoebox lid is fine)

Black crayon or marker

Scissors

Two ribbons, each about 18 inches (46 cm) long

Stapler

What to Do

1. Color the piece of cardboard black.
2. Cut out a little mask with slits for eyes.
3. Staple a ribbon to each side of your mask. Put the mask on and tie the ribbons together at the back of your head.
4. Go outside in the snow and find out how well your goggles work!

Brown Creeper

Did you find this bird on page 38? Creepers circle up tree trunks, hunting for insects. When they reach the top, they fly to the bottom of another tree and start up again. Creepers make their nests under bits of bark sticking out from the tree.

Red-breasted Nuthatch
This bird has a pale orange breast, a gray-blue back, a black cap, and a black stripe through its eyes. It nests in a hole in a tree, and spreads pitch, the sticky material that oozes from a pine tree, around the entrance.

Brrrrrd!
Most Winter Wrens fly south in winter, but sometimes a few birds tough it out in the north. This may be how the Winter Wren got its name. It's also called the Mouse Wren and the Spruce Wren.

Golden-crowned Kinglet
The Golden-crowned Kinglet is named for its yellow cap. The male also has an orange stripe on top of his head. Kinglets flutter their wings as they hop along branches looking for insects.

Black-capped Chickadee
Chickadees are often joined by other birds, such as nuthatches, kinglets, and creepers. In winter, you may see chickadees visiting bird feeders in your neighborhood.

Holiday Treats

It's an old custom in many snowy lands to feed birds during winter holidays. You can feed birds all winter by decorating an evergreen tree with strings of popcorn and raisins or other dried fruit.

Roll pinecones in a mixture of peanut butter and cornmeal and hang from branches. Hang orange halves, dog biscuits, doughnuts, pretzels, and peanuts from your tree, too. Watch them with your binoculars to see who visits. Record what you see. Here are some questions to get you started:

- How do different birds act while they eat? Do some hang upside down, like chickadees? Do others walk along the branches?

- Which birds eat while on the tree? Which birds snatch food and fly away with it?

- Do any birds try to chase away other kinds of birds?

- Are there any birds that eat crumbs off the ground underneath the tree?

Caw of the Wild

Crows and ravens are both big black birds. How can you tell them apart? One way is to note how the bird flies. Crows flap their wings and rarely glide. Ravens often glide and also swoop, soar, and even tumble through the air. Look at the tail, too. A raven's tail is shaped like a pointed shovel, or wedge. A crow's tail is shaped like a fan. Ravens are also bigger than crows with a heavier beak and a shaggy-looking throat.

Raven

Glossary

algae: Tiny non-flowering green plants.

antlers: Solid bone that grows in a pair from the head of a deer.

bacteria: Living things that have only one cell. Most bacteria are so tiny that millions can fit into one square inch (6.45 square cm).

binoculars: Two small telescopes placed side by side with a wheel or "seesaw" to bring what you are looking at into focus.

blind: A place where you can hide to look at animals without being seen.

coniferous: A kind of tree or bush that produces seeds in cones and usually does not lose all its leaves, or needles, in the fall.

covey: A small flock of birds.

crest: The feathers on a bird's head that stick up and come to a point.

dabble: To use a beak to reach for food in the bottom of shallow water. Ducks that do this are called "dabblers."

deciduous: A kind of tree or bush that loses its leaves in the fall and grows new ones to replace them in the spring.

field guide: A book with facts and pictures that is used to identify different kinds of animals, plants, rocks, shells, and other things in nature.

focus: To adjust binoculars or telescopes so you can clearly see whatever you are looking at.

habitat: The area in nature where a kind of plant or animal grows or lives.

hibernation: A period of inactivity, or a kind of sleep, during the winter. Some animals that hibernate are frogs, reptiles, and bears.

lard: A kind of animal fat sometimes used for cooking.

lens: The four pieces of curved glass (or plastic) in binoculars that you look through.

magnify: To make something look bigger than it really is.

magnification power: How many times bigger binoculars will make something faraway look than if you used just your own eyes.

map: A flat chart or diagram of an area.

marsh: A kind of freshwater wetland that contains standing water all year long.

meadow: An area of land that contains mostly grasses.

migrate: To move from one place to another.

mob: When several birds of one kind attack or harry one bird of another kind. For example, crows will often mob a hawk.

needles: The needle-shaped leaves of a pine tree or other conifer.

pitch: The resin, or sticky material, produced by pine trees and other conifers.

plankton: Tiny plants and animals that swim or float in open water.

quill: The sharp, stiff, hollow spine of a porcupine.

suet: Animal fat.

telescope: A long, rounded tool with lenses that magnify things that are far away.

Index

In wildness is the preservation of the world.

—Henry David Thoreau

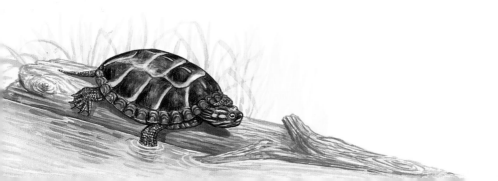